I0180909

First Published in 2025
Kindle Direct Publishing (UK Office)
44 Ashbourne Drive
Coxhoe
DH6 4SW

Edited by: Jamila Morrison (UK)
Claudette Leckie (USA)

Mother Hen is one of several hens living on a farm owned by Farmer John, his wife Wilma, and their three children: Danny, Janie and Ricky. There are other animals on the farm including Shaggy and Snappy, the two Pembroke Welsh Corgi dogs and Whiskers the Japanese Bobtail cat.

The children love to help their parents on the farm, especially when it is time to feed the hens. Mother Hen is their favourite. She is very friendly and playful; the children love her. Making lots of memories on the farm, Mother Hen has been with them since she was a tiny chick.

One day Farmer John said to Mrs John: "It's time for Mother Hen to sit on her eggs and give us some chicks. She has been showing signs that she is ready. We haven't had much luck with the other hens, because of the hawks, mongooses, foxes and other neighbouring farm animals.

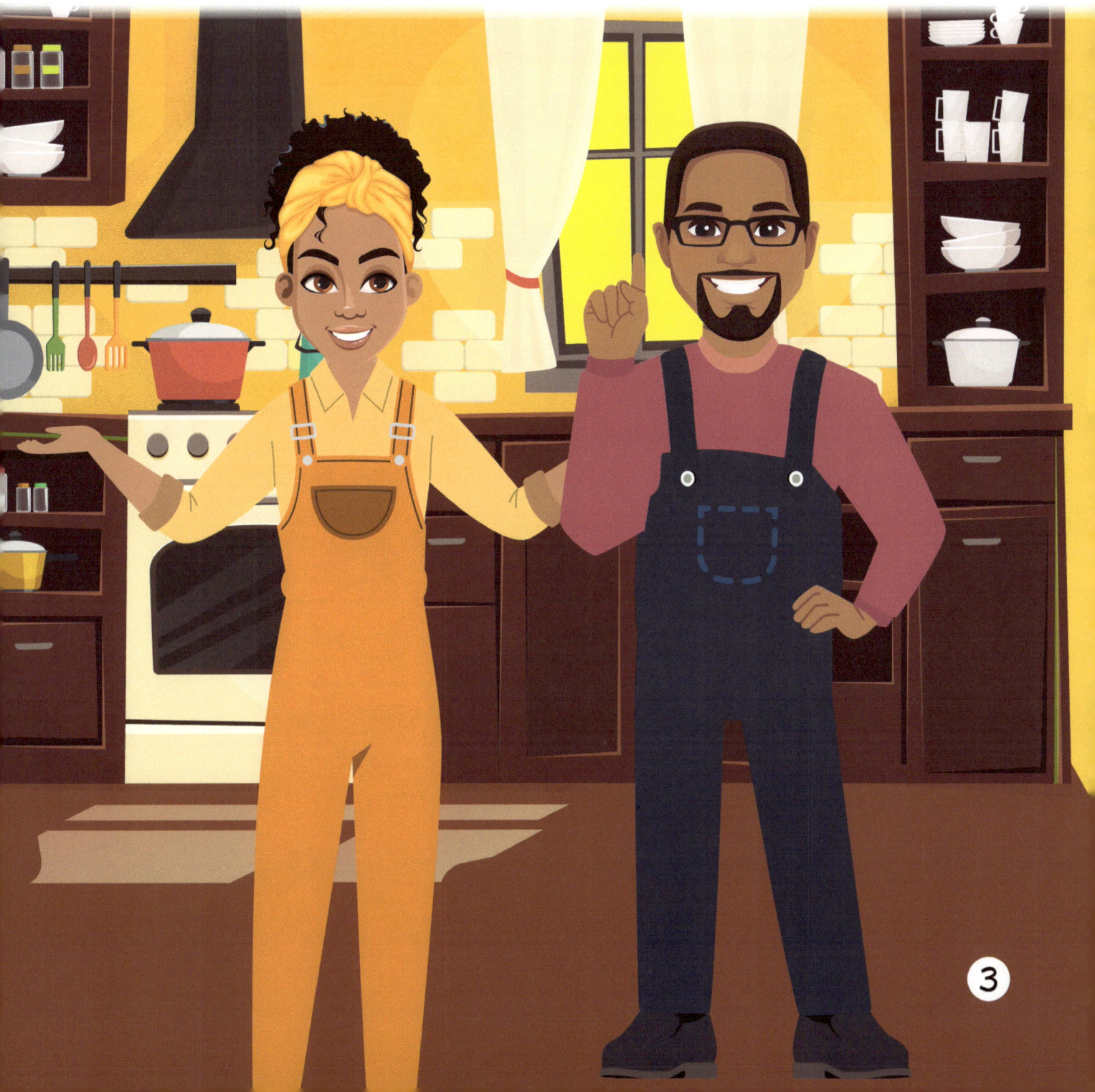

Mother Hen had been nesting on her eggs for days and as a result, she is very protective. She would get very cross if anyone ventured too close to her nest or tried to touch her eggs.

Farmer John warned the children, "do not go near Mother Hen while she is waiting for her chicks to hatch."
Despite the warning, Ricky, the youngest child, did not listen to his father, and went to the hens' house. As soon as he saw Mother Hen, he ran over to get her attention.

Mother Hen was sitting quietly in her nest when she heard a rustling sound. Looking up she saw the boy and before he could get too close, Mother Hen squawked at him for disturbing her. Startled, Ricky ran out crying, he had never seen Mother Hen like that before.

When Farmer John saw Ricky's sad face, he asked "what happened?".
With a sad face he related the incident to Farmer John. Farmer John
was really upset with Ricky.
"I told you not to go near the hens' house, while Mother Hen is waiting
for her chicks to hatch", he scolded.
"But dad" cried Ricky "you always go into the hens' house."
"Yes," said Farmer John, but I do so to clean the hen house and feed
her." He sighed, then said, "Next time you can come and help me feed
her, but do not touch her."
"Okay" stated Ricky, feeling much better.

Meanwhile, Mother Hen was worried. "Are those humans trying to steal my eggs? She wondered. "Oh, I'm not leaving this nest. I'm sure the farmer will continue bringing me food and water, but he is not having any of my chicks. And that boy, why did he come inside?" Mother Hen was getting very suspicious.

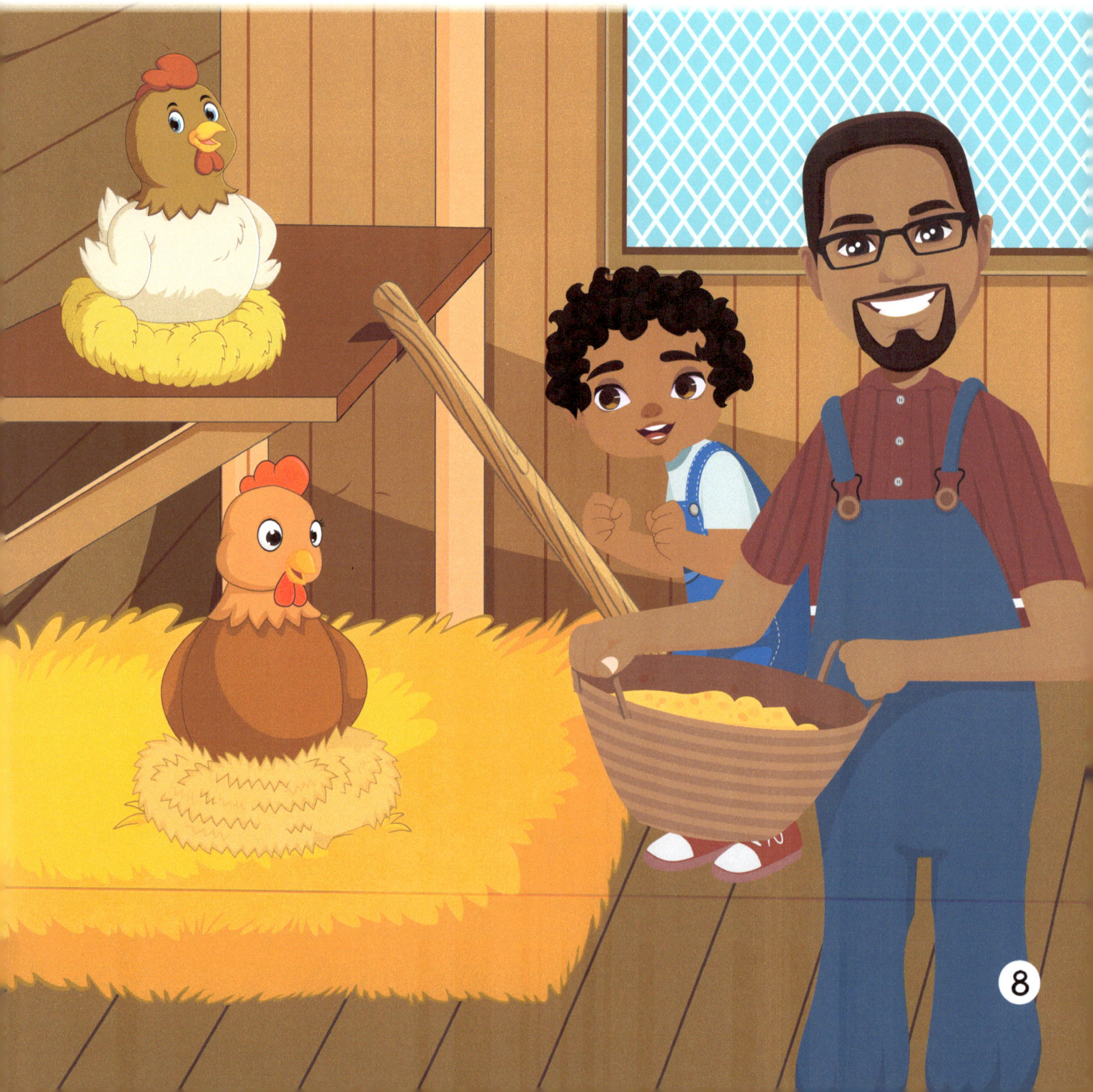

Days passed. Mother Hen had been sitting on her eggs for over two weeks, and she was getting tired, nothing was happening. Then suddenly, she heard a crack. The eggs started hatching!

After a few hours, Mother Hen had all her twelve chicks. She made a loud clucking noise, to signal that she was a very happy and proud hen.

Farmer John and Mrs. John ran to the hens' house when they heard Mother Hen cluck. They were surprised that all twelve eggs had been hatched. Mother Hen was overjoyed with her twelve beautiful chicks.

Afterwards, Farmer John and Mrs. John discussed how they would protect Mother Hen and her twelve chicks.
Just then, excitable screams could be heard from the children, as they came running in to see the new chicks.

Mother Hen was still very protective of her chicks, and once again scowled at the children.

The children then scrambled out of the hens' house with flustered faces. Since Mother Hen was their favourite hen, they were shocked to see her so agitated.

Farmer John said to the kids "don't worry about Mother Hen, she is very protective of her chicks, just like all human mothers are protective of their new-born."

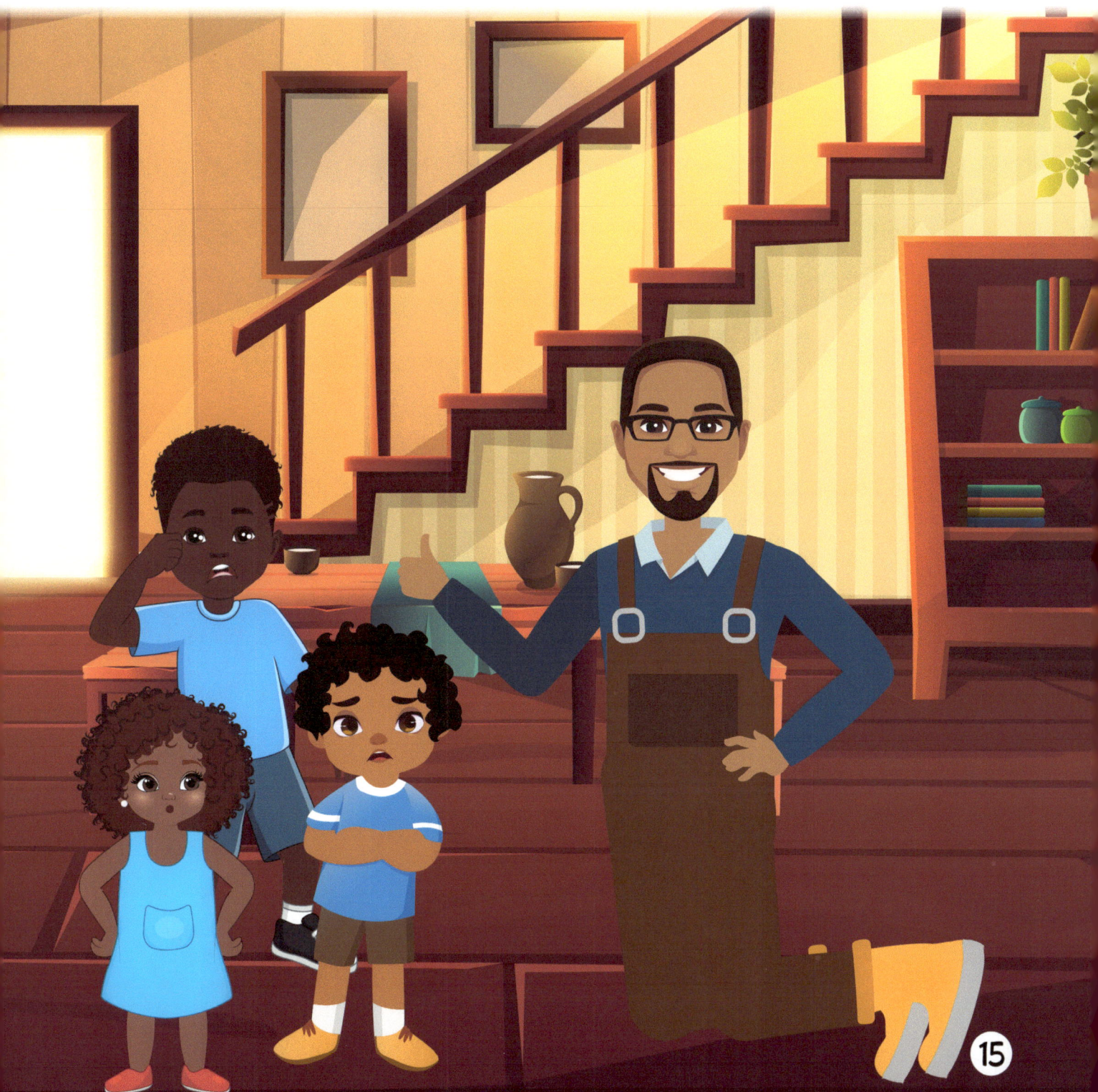

Farmer John then continued to say to Danny, Janie and Ricky:
"we must try to protect her and the chicks from the hawks,
foxes and the mongooses, because they will eat her chicks, and
we do not want that to happen."

The next day, Farmer John decided to make a special coop inside the hens' house, specifically for Mother Hen and her twelve chicks. This way they would be safe from predators.

Mother Hen was very proud of her chicks, she counted them one... two...
three... and there were twelve chicks.
Mother Hen walked around the farmyard with her twelve chicks all beside
her. She kept a watchful eye on everyone around the farmyard.

Some of the other hens were staring at her. Some seemed genuinely happy for her, while others were saying that she would not be able to keep them all and that they would either be eaten or taken away.

Mother Hen continued to proudly walk around the farmyard, until she saw Shelia the Red Hen. Sheila had ten chicks, but only five survived. I wonder what happened, Mother Hen quipped. Sheila the Red Hen said with tears in her eyes, "they wandered off when I wasn't looking, and only five of them came back. I think they were eaten by either the hawks, foxes, mongooses, or maybe the humans took them for their own, or sold them at the market".

Mother Hen had heard the humans talk about the hawks, foxes, and the mongoose. She agreed that they were horrible creatures who may have eaten at Shelia's chicks and some of the other hens on the farm. Because of this, some of the hens were in distress. Mother Hen went over and said a few kind words to the hens, then continued her walk.

"I won't walk too far from the farm," Mother Hen said to herself. She thought about her little ones and their frisky behaviour whenever they wandered outside.

The twelve chicks had a habit of getting into mischief. She didn't like them playing with the cat either, since he plays too roughly with them.

Farmer John, Mrs. John, and two of their neighbours: Sam and Mary, came over to help build the special hen's house for Mother Hen and the chicks.

Farmer John knew that if they did not try to protect Mother Hen and the chicks, they would fall prey to predators. That was the one thing he did not want.

Mrs. John said to Farmer John, "it is going to be a hard task to get her into the hen's house with the chicks. We must get her in first, then it would be easier for us to catch the little chicks."

Farmer John knew that Mother Hen could be extremely cross when she's cooped up, but he also knew it was for her own protection. Mother Hen then started pecking at them, thinking that they were going to steal her chicks. She pecked farmer Sam on his hand, but he was wearing gloves, so he didn't feel anything.

Eventually, with lots of struggles, the farmers placed Mother Hen in the special chicken coop with Mother Hen still angrily clucking at them. Afterwards, Farmer John said to the children, "you can all help by gathering up the little chicks and placing them with Mother Hen. However, be incredibly careful when you do.

The children counted all twelve chicks.
Afterwards, Ricky exclaimed: "we should give them all names."
"Don't be silly" said his big brother Danny, "they will be sold to the
market when they are much bigger", or "be eaten by Predators" said
Janie smiling.
"Okay children, enough of that," said Farmer John.

Farmer John placed the chicks with Mother Hen and secured the chicken coop, by setting up a bell on the latch for any intruders, so he could hear it from inside the house.

"You and your chicks are safe Mother Hen," said Farmer John smiling. Although she was still agitated, she looked at the tired little faces on her chicks as they all settled under her wing to sleep. She thought, "I'll let it slide for today."

Farmer John gave one last look at Mother Hen and her chicks. He smiled at their faces and went back to the house to rejoin the rest of his family.

THE END

www.ingramcontent.com/pod-product-compliance
Lightning Source LLC
LaVergne TN
LVHW072115070426
835510LV00002B/65